D1233468

Endangered DESERT ANIMALS

Marie Allgor

New York

Published in 2013 by The Rosen Publishing Group, Inc.
29 East 21st Street, New York, NY 10010

First Edition

Editor: Jennifer Way
Book Design: Julio Gil

Photo Credits: Cover Pichugin Dmitry/Shutterstock.com; pp. 4, 11 RF_CD Geo Atlas; p. 5 Patrick Poendl/Shutterstock.com; pp. 6–7 F.C.G./Shutterstock.com; p. 7 Brenda Carson/Shutterstock.com; p. 8 Gregory MD./Photo Researchers/Getty Images; p. 9 (main) Anthony Mercieca/Photo Researchers/Getty Images; p. 9 (inset) Attila Jandi/Shutterstock.com; pp. 10, 17 (main), 21 (inset) iStockphoto/Thinkstock; p. 11 Hemera/Thinkstock; p. 12 © FLPA/Frank W. Lane/Age Fotostock; p. 13 AISPIX/Shutterstock.com; p. 14 Mitalpatel/Shutterstock.com; p. 15 Critterbiz/Shutterstock.com; p. 16 Max Allen/Shutterstock.com; p. 17 (inset) S.J. Krasemann/Peter Arnold/Getty Images; p. 18 Noo/Shutterstock.com; p. 19 Nagel Photography/Shutterstock.com; p. 20 Matt Jeppson/Shutterstock.com; p. 21 (main) Jason Mintzer/Shutterstock.com; p. 22 Darul Faust/Shutterstock.com.

Library of Congress Cataloging-in-Publication Data

Allgor, Marie.
Endangered desert animals / by Marie Allgor. — 1st ed.
p. cm. — (Save Earth's animals!)
Includes index.
ISBN 978-1-4488-7423-1 (library binding) — ISBN 978-1-4488-7496-5 (pbk.) —
ISBN 978-1-4488-7570-2 (6-pack)
1. Endangered species—Juvenile literature. 2. Desert animals—Juvenile literature. 3. Desert ecology—Juvenile literature. 4. Wildlife conservation—Juvenile literature. I. Title.
QL83.A438 2013
591.68—dc23

2011051875

Manufactured in China

CPSIA Compliance Information: Batch # CS12PK: For Further Information contact Rosen Publishing, New York, New York at 1-800-237-9932

Contents

Welcome to the Desert!

The world is home to countless living things. Some of these living things need warm, wet places to live. Others need cool and dry places. There are several different **biomes** on Earth. These big areas are defined by their weather and the kinds of plants

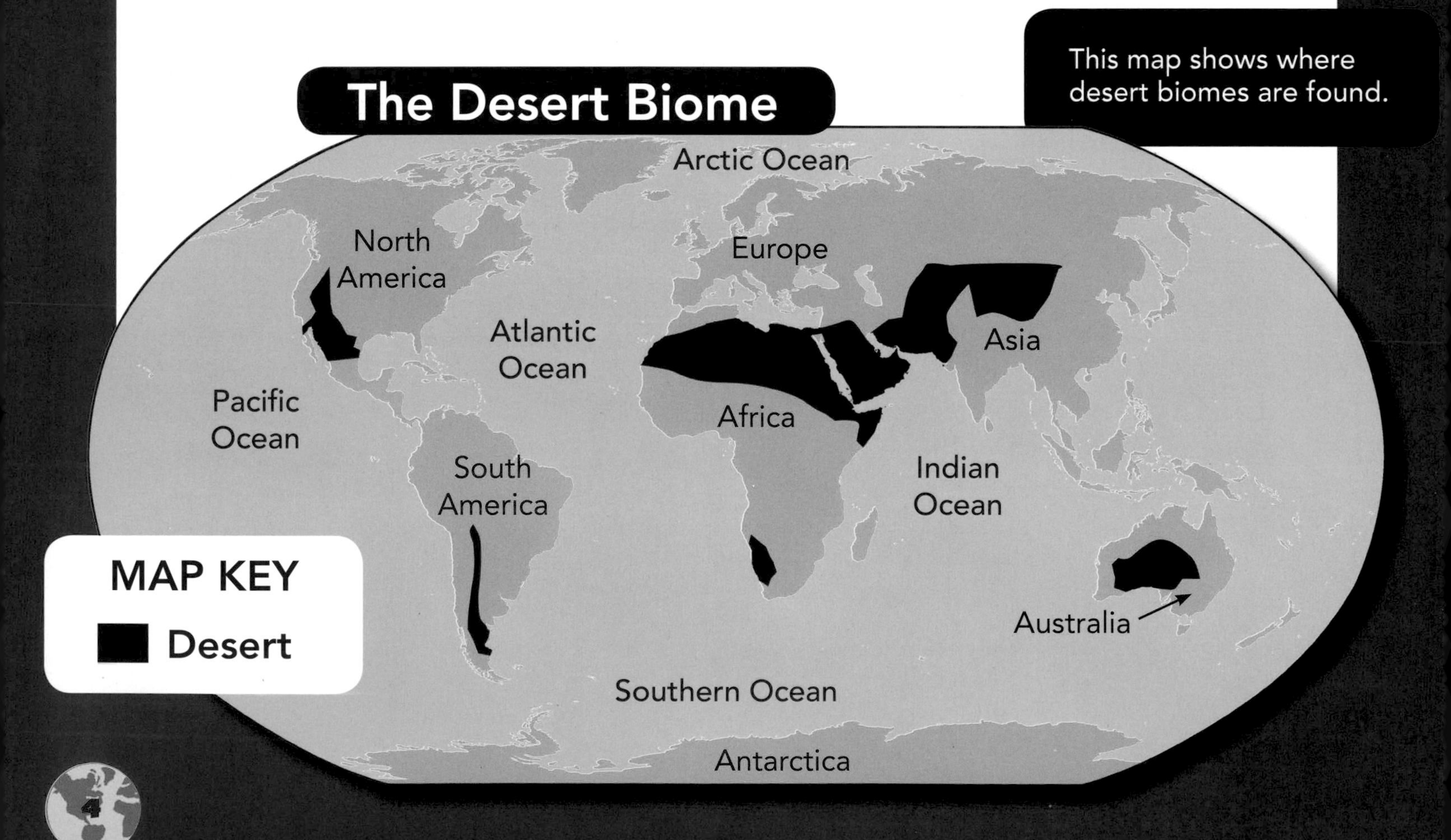

This map shows where desert biomes are found.

Camels are desert animals. There are two kinds of camels, Bactrian and dromedary. These are dromedary camels.

and animals that live there. The ocean is a biome. The forest is a biome, too.

The desert biome makes up one-fifth of Earth's surface. Deserts do not get a lot of **precipitation**. This makes them hard places to live. Many animals there are **endangered**. This book will introduce you to some of the desert's endangered animals.

Desert Climate

There are many kinds of deserts, including hot and cold deserts. One thing they all have in common is that they are dry. To be called a desert, a place must get fewer than 20 inches (50 cm) of precipitation each year.

Monument Valley, shown here, is a desert area in the states of Arizona and Utah.

Coyotes are found throughout North America. Some coyotes live in the desert.

Hot deserts are warm all year and can get as hot as 120° F (49° C) in the summer. The Chihuahuan, Sonoran, and Mojave are all hot, dry deserts in North America.

Cold deserts include the Atacama Desert, in South America, and the Gobi, in Asia. These deserts can be as cold as -40° F (-40° C) in the winter.

Habitats in the Desert

Deserts may not get a lot of rainfall, but they can be rich **habitats** for plenty of plants and animals. Low shrubs, short trees, and cacti are the main plants in hot deserts. Reptiles, lizards, small mammals, birds, and insects live there, too.

The deathstalker scorpion lives in the deserts of North Africa and the Middle East. It gets its name because it is the world's deadliest scorpion!

The desert kangaroo rat lives throughout North America's deserts.

Small, thick-leaved plants like this one store water in their leaves. This adaptation helps it live in the dry areas of Morocco in which it grows.

Many desert animals have special **adaptations** that let them live in their dry, hot homes. Some animals, such as camels, are able to get by without drinking a lot of water. Other animals come out mainly at night when the air is cooler.

The Desert's Endangered Animals

Deserts are home to many plants and animals, but this does not mean deserts are easy places to live. Many animal species in deserts are in trouble. The animals on these pages are endangered and could soon be **extinct**.

MAP KEY

- Slender-Horned Gazelle
- Bactrian Camel
- Desert Tortoise
- Nelson's Antelope Squirrel
- Egyptian Vulture

Egyptian Vulture

1. Slender-Horned Gazelle

Scientists **estimate** that there are fewer than 2,500 slender-horned gazelles left in the wild. This animal is also called the rhim gazelle.

2. Egyptian Vulture

There are thought to be fewer than 40,000 Egyptian vultures left in the world. This may sound like a lot, but in many places more than half the population has died.

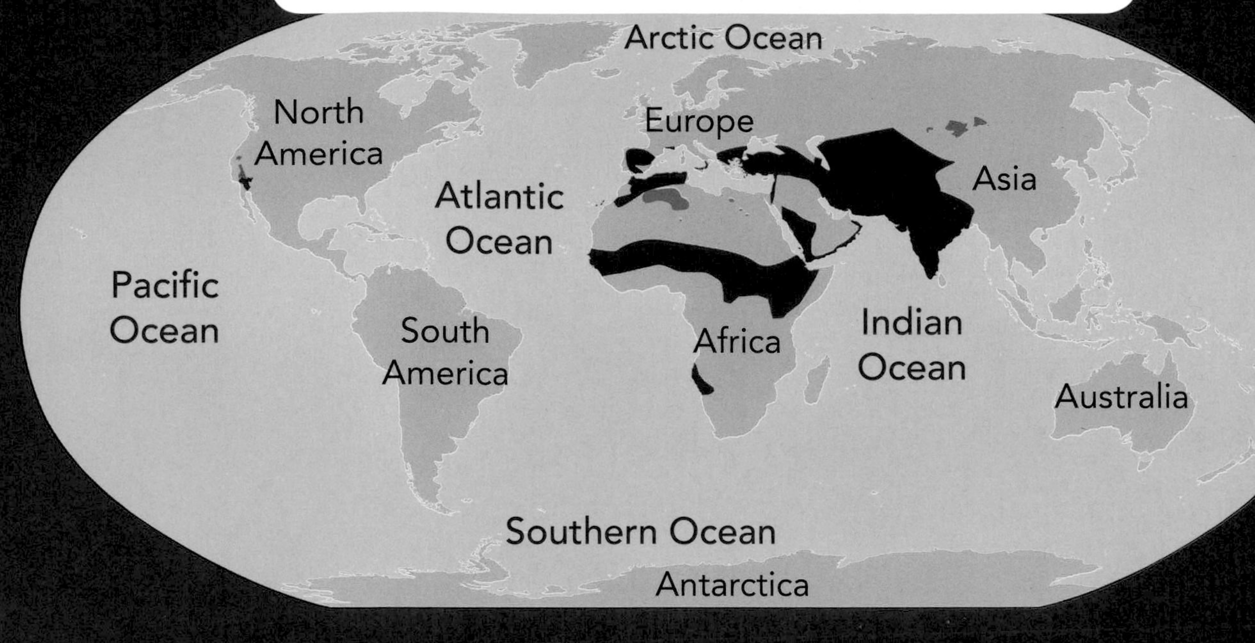

3. Nelson's Antelope Squirrel

The Nelson's antelope squirrel is also called the San Joaquin antelope squirrel. This squirrel is endangered because it has lost more than 80 percent of its habitat.

4. Bactrian Camel

There are only about 1,000 Bactrian camels in the wild. This species is critically endangered.

5. Desert Tortoise

The desert tortoise population is 90 percent smaller than it was in the 1950s. The desert tortoise is listed as threatened. This means that if things do not change, it will be endangered very soon.

Slender-Horned Gazelle

The slender-horned gazelle roams widely across the Sahara as it looks for food. It likes the parts of the desert with large dunes best. It is thought that these animals were plentiful up until 10 years ago. Since then, their numbers have dropped quickly due to too much hunting. The total number of these gazelles is guessed to be fewer than 2,500.

The slender-horned gazelle has a light coat that helps reflect the Sun's heat away from the animal. This one lives in a zoo.

The African wild dog hunts gazelles, including the slender-horned gazelle. This wild dog is endangered, too.

The main danger to the slender-horned gazelle is overhunting and poaching in protected places. **Climate change** and habitat loss hurting the plants it eats is also a problem.

Egyptian Vulture

The Egyptian vulture nests in caves or on rocky outcrops and low cliffs. It lives not just in Egypt, but in many places throughout North Africa, the Middle East, Asia, and Europe. It is listed as endangered because its numbers have dropped so quickly

The Egyptian vulture travels across a wide range, so its population is spread thinly.

The golden eagle, shown here, often hunts young Egyptian vultures.

in the past 40 years. In Europe, the population went down by more than half.

Some of the dangers to the Egyptian vulture include electrocution by power lines and poisoning. There are also fewer dead animals being left on roadsides and other places where the birds can eat them.

Nelson's Antelope Squirrel

The Nelson's antelope squirrel is a ground squirrel that lives in California, mainly in the central and western San Joaquin Valley. These animals like dry scrublands and live in burrows they borrow from other animals. They eat mostly green plants, grass seeds, and insects.

The American badger is found throughout central and western North America. It preys on small mammals like the Nelson's antelope squirrel.

The Nelson's antelope squirrel lives in scrubby desert areas and grasslands in southern California.

Nelson's antelope squirrels live in small groups, called colonies. A colony has about eight members in it.

Scientists think there could be between 124,000 and 413,000 Nelson's antelope squirrels left. Their habitat has been taken over for farmland, roads, housing, and businesses. Oil drilling has also hurt their habitat. Luckily, laws are being passed to set aside land for these squirrels. Hopefully, this will be enough to save these animals from extinction.

Bactrian Camel

There are about 14 million camels in the world. Most of these are **domesticated** dromedary camels. Bactrian camels are wild camels that live in the Gobi, a desert in Mongolia and China.

Wild Bactrians are critically endangered. These animals are in danger from hunting by people and

Bactrian camels have adapted to the cold temperatures in the Gobi by growing thick, shaggy fur in the winter. They shed this fur when it gets warmer.

Long eyelashes help keep blowing sand out of the Bactrian camel's eyes.

wolves. They are also in danger from habitat loss as domesticated camels take over the places where the wild camels live. Land has been put aside to protect these camels. Captive breeding programs have also been started. Let's hope these measures work!

Desert Tortoise

Desert tortoises live in the Mojave and Sonoran deserts of southern California, Nevada, and Utah. They eat herbs, grasses, wildflowers, shrubs, and cacti. This tortoise spends most of its time underground. This helps it stay safe from the 120° F (49° C) summer heat!

The desert tortoise gets most of its water from the plants it eats. It can go for a year without drinking water!

The Gila monster, shown here, is a lizard that preys on desert tortoise eggs and young tortoises.

The desert tortoise's front legs have sharp scales that help it dig burrows.

The number of desert tortoises has dropped by 90 percent in the past 50 years. Scientists think that there are only about 100,000 desert tortoises left in the wild. These tortoises do not do well near people. People disturb their habitat and hunt them. Climate change is also hurting desert tortoises. Time will tell if conservation efforts are working.

Save the Desert's Animals!

Deserts are the perfect home for animals like camels and desert tortoises. If we take away or hurt their habitats, though, then we are hurting these animals.

The Sonoran Desert is found in the southwestern United States and in northwestern Mexico. This large desert contains several protected areas.

It might seem like it would not matter if deserts got any hotter or drier than they are. This is not true. Climate change upsets the balance of desert life. Laws are in place to protect many desert places. It is our job to help endangered desert animals so that we do not lose these important species.

Glossary

ADAPTATIONS (a-dap-TAY-shunz) Changes in an animal that helps it stay alive.

BIOMES (BY-ohmz) Kinds of places with certain weather patterns and kinds of plants.

CLIMATE CHANGE (KLY-mut CHAYNJ) Changes in Earth's weather that was caused by things people did.

CRITICALLY (KRIH-tih-kuh-lee) Being at a turning point.

DOMESTICATED (duh-MES-tih-kayt-ed) Raised to live with people.

ENDANGERED (in-DAYN-jerd) In danger of no longer existing.

ESTIMATE (ES-teh-mayt) To make a guess based on knowledge or facts.

EXTINCT (ik-STINGKT) No longer existing.

HABITATS (HA-buh-tats) The surroundings where animals or plants naturally live.

PRECIPITATION (preh-sih-pih-TAY-shun) Any moisture that falls from the sky. Rain and snow are precipitation.

Index

Websites

Due to the changing nature of Internet links, PowerKids Press has developed an online list of websites related to the subject of this book. This site is updated regularly. Please use this link to access the list: www.powerkidslinks.com/sea/desert/